詩的五重奏

MY SELECTED POEMS
IN 5 LANGUAGES
MES POEMES SELECTIONNES
EN 5 LANGUES
MEINE AUSGEWÄHLTEN GEDICHTE
IN 5 SPRACHEN
VÁLOGATOTT
KÖLTEMÉNYEIM
5 NYELVEN

徐 世 澤 著
DR. HSU SHIH-TZE
(Stephen Shihtze Hsu)

文史哲出版社印行
Liberal Arts Press
MAY, 1998

國家圖書館出版品預行編目資料

詩的五重奏 = My selected poems in 5
languages = Mes poêmes séléctionnés en 5
langues / 徐世澤著. -- 初版. - 臺北市：
文史哲，民 87
面 ； 公分. - (文史哲詩叢 ; 29)
ISBN 957-549-145-9 (平裝)

851.486   87006576

文史哲詩叢 ㉙

詩的五重奏

著　　者：徐　　世　　澤
出版者：文　史　哲　出　版　社
登記證字號：行政院新聞局版臺業字五三三七號
發行人：彭　　正　　雄
發行所：文　史　哲　出　版　社
印刷者：文　史　哲　出　版　社
臺北市羅斯福路一段七十二巷四號
郵政劃撥帳號：一六一八〇一七五
電話 886-2-23511028・傳眞 886-2-23965656

實價新臺幣一八〇元

中　華　民　國　八　十　七　年　五　月　初　版

MY SELECTED POEMS IN 5 LANGUAGES

Copyright @   : Dr. HSU SHIH-TZE

Author   : Stephen Shihtzu Hsu

Copy-editor   : Dr. Imre P. Zsoldos

Publisher   : Liberal Arts Press

Printery   : Liberal Arts Press

Address   : 4 Lane 72 Roosevelt Road

                 Section 1, Taipei , Taiwan

                 Republic of China

Telephone   : 886-2-23511028

Fax   : 886-2-23965656

Price   : U.S. $5.50

First Edition , May 1, 1998

韓　序

　　就我所知，現代醫師能寫舊體詩詞與新詩者極少，徐世澤醫師應是其中之一。徐醫師善用通俗文句和科技名詞入詩，令人讀來感受良深。

　　聞旅台之外籍教授及學生多人，喜讀其詩，我甚感興奮，今見其中英對照詩集出版，乃欣為之序。

韓韶華博士

國立陽明大學前校長

1991年5月10日

Preface

To the best of my knowledge, in our days, few physicians can write old verses as well as modern poetry. Doctor Hsu Shih-Tze is a rare one that we can find. He adopts popular phrases and technical terms in poems that move us deeply.

Having heard that many foreign professors and students who stay in Taiwan have special enthusiasm for his poems, I feel very much amazed. It is a great pleasure to see that his English-Chinese Anthology has been put into print.

May 10,1991

Shou-Hwa Han,M.D.,Ph.D.

President

National Yang Ming University,

Préface

Autant que je sache, de nos jours, peu de médecins peuvent écrire des poèmes classiques aussi bien que des vers libres. Dr. Hsu Shih- Tze en est une exception faisant rareté. Il adopte les locutions populaires et les termes techniques au temps contemporain. Cela nous touche profondément.

Ayant entendu que nombreux professeurs et étudiants étrangers qui habitent à Taiwan, ont un enthousiasme particulier pour ses poèmes, je m'en réjouis beaucoup. C'est un grand plaisir pour moi de voir que cette Anthologie Chinoise-Anglaise ait pu être publiée.

le lo mai,1991

Dr. Shou-Hwa Han
Yang-Ming University,
Recteur Magnifique

Einleitungsworte

So weit es mir bekannt ist, in unseren Tagen können nur sehr wenige Ärzte klassische und moderne Dichtungen in gleicher Zeit schreiben. Dr. Hsu Shih-Tze ist einer von solchen Ärzten, den wir noch finden können. Er adoptiert populäre Sprüche und technische Ausdrücke zu unserer Epoch in seinen Dichtungen, die uns tief berühren.

Weil ich gehört habe, dass viele ausländische Professoren und Studenten, die sich in Taiwan weilen, für seine Dichtungen sehr begeistert sind, freue ich mich sehr. Es ist eine grosse Freude für mich diese Englisch- Chinesische Anthologie gedruckt gehabt zu sehen.

Am 10 -ten Mai, 1991

> Dr. Shou-Hwa Han
> Yang Ming Universität,
> Rektor

Ajánló sorok

Ha jól tudom, napjainkban kevés orvos van (Tajvanban), aki egyaránt költ klasszikus költeményeket és szabad verselésben megírt költeményeket.

Dr. Hsü kivételes egyén ebben, ritkaságnak számít. Adoptálja a népi mondásokat és terminusz technikuszokat korunkra. Ezzel mély húrokat pendít meg bennünk.

Miután hallottam számos tanártól és külföldi diáktól, akik Tajvanban élnek, hogy rendkívül lelkesednek a költeményeiért, nagyon örülök, jó-magam is. Nagyon nagy boldogság számomra látni ennek a kínai-angol antológiának a kiadását.

1991 május 10-én.

Dr. Shou-Hwa Han
Yang Ming Orvostudományi Egyetem,
Rektor

賀徐世澤醫師榮膺二屆詩人節優秀詩人，
詩運獎誌慶兼題其「養生吟」，并廣贈國
際詩人。

詩壇優秀開詩運
更有吟眸展五洲
擒藻寰中長有抱
養生天下永無憂
千秋亙古人文耀
兩岸於今韻事酬
一卷流傳期化俗
杏林日暖縱優遊
何岳七月二日

Congratulations to Dr. Hsu for his Chinese-English Anthology

The world's poets are united in Taiwan for a Congress.

They came from every continent and far-away places.

Dr. Hsu's "Regimen" is as deep as the ocean.

His poetical eyes can leer even at the invisible,

What common people cannot see.

Many generations to come will be helped by them to think deeper.

In our days, poets are looked upon as superior beings,

Supermen and superwomen.

Mainland China and Taiwan have mutual cultural communications.

This "Regimen" can develop social customs

In medical circles and put in movement

High waves in the sea of poetry,

And like the sun, warm up the earth.

July 2, 1992

Dr. Imre Prince Zsoldos svd.

Félicitations à Dr.Hsu à la parution de son Anthologie Chinoise-Anglaise

Les poètes du monde sont réunis pour un congrès á Taïpei, venant des cinq continents, de très loin et de tout près.

Ce "Régime" est profond comme la mer ou l'océan. Les yeux de ce poète sont perspicaces; voient même l'invisible très clair, même ce que ne voit pas un mortel ordinaire...

L'Anthologie aidera les générations à venir à penser plus profondément.

De nos jours, les poètes sont considérés comme des supermen.

La Chine et Taïwan ont une culture commune et mutuelle.

Cette Anthologie veut aider à développer la civilité, les coutumes dans les cercles médicaux et lancer un mouvement comme les vagues de la mer dans l'océan des poètes, et être un peu comme le soleil pour nous réchauffer la terre.

Le 2 juillet 1992

Dr.Ime Prince Zsoldos svd

Glückwünsche an Dr.Hsu für die Erscheinung seiner chinesisch-englischen Anthologie.

Die Dichter der Welt sind in Taipei für einen Kongress versammelt.

Die fünf Kontinente der ganzen Erde haben Representante gesandt.

Dr Hsu's Buch, das "Regimen" ist so tief wie der Ozean.

Mit seinen scharfsinnigen Augen sieht er auch das Unsichtbare und auch das, was ein gewönlicher Mensch nicht sehen kann.

Er wird die künftigen Generazionen dazu helfen, dass sie tiefer denken können. Unsere Epoche nennt die Dichter Supermen.

Taiwan und China haben gemeinde, gegenseitige Kulturquellen.

Diese Publikation soll dazu helfen, dass diese Kultur gepflegt wird mitten unten den medizinischen Kreisen. Sie sollte wie die Wellen des Ozeans, die Dichter in Bewegung setzen, um dasselbe zu tun und wie eine Art von Sonne unsere Erde ein klein wenig erwärmen.

Den 2ten Juli 1992   Dr. Imre P. Zsoldos svd

Gratuláció Dr.Hsunek a kínai-angol antológiájahoz.

Kongresszusra jöttek össze a világ költői Tajvanba.

Képviselteti magát földünk minden kontinense, tája.

Dr. Hsu "Életrendje" mély mint az oceánok árka...

Éles költő szemével a láthatatlant is átfúrja, vizsgálja,

Azt is, amit a közönséges ember nem, vagy alig látja.

Jövő nemzedékeket serkent majd mély gondolkodásra.

Korunk a költőket igen nagy szuperembereknek titulálja.

Tajvannak és Kínának kölcsönös a kulturá lis múltja.

Az "Életrend" erre tanit, erre int, ezt fejleszti, ezt ápolja

verseivel az orvosok közt. Tengehullámként hat ez a munka.

S mint a nap a földünket átforrosítja, bearanyozza.

1992 július 2.   Dr. Zsoldos Imre P. svd.

詩的五重奏

目　次

Contents
Table de matières
Inhalt
Tartalom

韓　序 ················· 5

Preface ················· 6

Préface ················· 7

Einleitungsworte ················· 8

Bevezetés, ajánló sorok ················· 9

賀徐世澤醫師榮膺運獎兼題其「養生吟」················· 10

Congratulations to Dr. Hsu for his Chinese-English
Anthology ················· 11

Félicitations à Dr.Hsu à la parution de son Anthologie Chinoise-Anglaise ················· 12

Glückwünsche an Dr. Hsu für die Erscheinung seiner
chinesisch-englischen Anthologie. ················· 13

Gratuláció Dr.Hsunek a kínai-angol antológiájához ········ 14

目　錄 ·· 15

Note ··· 19

1.鴻　福？ ··· 21

Boundless Bliss·· 22

Bonheur bien beau ? ·· 23

Is es wirklich ein unendiches Glück ? ··················· 24

Mi a határtalan boldogság ? ································· 25

2.賀趙德恕博士(Dr. Zsoldos)六十華誕······················ 26

To The Very Reverend Imre P. Zsoldos,

Dean of Fujen Catholic University's

French Graduate School, on his 60th birthday.

·· 27

Félicitations au Révérend Père Imre P.Zsoldos svd.

Directeur de l'Institut de Français à l'université

FuJen, à l'occasion de son 60e anniversaire. ·········· 28

Dem Hochwürdigen Imre P.Zsoldos svd.

Direktor dees Französischen Institutes,

der katolischen Universität Fujen,

zu seinem 60-sten Geburtstag ······························ 29

Gratulació P. Zsoldos Imre svd atyának, Fuzsen

katolikus egyetem francia tanszékvezető tanárának

60-ik születésnapjára·· 30

3.颱　風(一) ·· 31

Typhoon (I) ·· 32

Thyphon (I) ·· 33

Taifun (I)·· 34'

Tifon (I) ·· 35

4. 颱　風㈡ ·· 36

Typhoon (II) ·· 37

Thyphon (II) ·· 38

Taifun (II)·· 39

Tifon (II) ·· 40

5. 颱　風㈢ ·· 41

Typhoon (III) ·· 42

Thyphon (III) ·· 43

Taifun　(III)·· 44

Tifon　(III) ·· 45

6. 贈 Dr. Zsoldos ·· 46

To Dr. Zsoldos ·· 47

Au Dr. Zsoldos ·· 48

An Dr. Zsoldos ·· 49

Dr. Zsoldosnak ·· 50

7. 白衣天使 ·· 51

The Nurse·· 52

L'infirmière ·· 53

Die Krankepflägerin·· 54

A nővérke·· 55

8.傳　情 ·· 56

　Communication of Love ····································· 57

　Communication de l'amour ······························· 58

　Mitteilung der Liebe ·· 59

　Szeretet közlés ·· 60

9.生與死 ·· 61

　Birth and Death ··· 62

　Vie et Mort ·· 63

　Leben und Tod ··· 64

　Élet és Halál ··· 65

10.榮總清晨 ·· 66

　Early Morning in Veterans General Hospital ········· 67

　Dans l'hôpital des vétérans ······························· 68

　In dem Spital der Veteraner ······························ 69

　Kora reggel a veteránok közkórházában ················ 70

11.重　逢 ·· 71

　Meet Again ·· 72

　Nouvelle Rencontre ··· 73

　Neue Begegnung ··· 74

　Újratalálkozás ··· 75

12.眞　情 ·· 76

　Deep Affection ·· 77

　Affection profonde ·· 78

　Tiefe Gefühle ·· 79

Hogy mély maradjon a szeretet················ 80

13.老詩人吟 ······································ 81

　Old Poet ······································ 82

　Vieux poète···································· 83

　Alter Dichter·································· 84

　Öreg költő ···································· 85

14.單　戀 ·· 86

　Unilateral Love································ 87

　Amour unilateral ······························ 88

　Einseitige Liebe ······························ 89

　Egyoldalú szertetet···························· 90

A study of the Tang Poetry by Stephen Shihtze Hsu········ 94

作者小傳 ·· 98

Introduction of Dr. Hsu Shih-tze ················ 100

Biographie de Dr. Hsu Shih-Tze ·················· 101

Biographie von Dr. Hsu Shih-Tze ················ 102

Dr.Hsu Hsu-Shih-Tze életrajza··················· 104

彩　照 ·· 105

後記及感謝語 ···································· 113

Postscript ······································ 114

Epilogue ·· 115

Nachwort ·· 116

Epilogus ·· 117

Note:

The English, French, German and Hungarian rendering of the Chinese poems was done by Dr. Imre P. Zsoldos svd.

Note:

La traduction des poèmes chinois en anglais, français, allemand et hongrois a été efféctuée par Dr.Imre P.Zsoldos svd.

Bemerkung

Die Übersetzung der chinesischen Dichtungen ins Englische, Französische, Deutsche und Ungarische wurde von Dr.Imre P.Zsoldos svd. getan.

Megjegyzés:

A kínai költeményeket Dr.Zsoldos Imre P. svd. forditotta angolra, franciara, németre és magyarra.

鴻　福？

人言長壽是鴻福？
長壽老人甚覺孤；
照顧起居防跌倒，
一人長壽兩人扶。

BOUNDLESS BLISS ?

Is it a boundless bliss when one lives till eighty ?

But an old man must always face sour solitude.

He must be taken care of, to prevent stumbling,

Two men have to back him up when he is so ageing.

Bonheur bien beau ?

Est-ce un bonbeur bien beau d'avoir 80 ans ?

La solitude y devient pesante cependant.

Quelqu'un doit 1' épauler continuellement.

Un viellard porte son ombre tout le temps.

Ist es wirlich ein unendliches Glück?

Ist es wirklich ein unendliches Glück, dass man achtzig Jahre alt wird ?

Aber ein alter Mann muss immer mit Einsamkeit kämpfen.

Er braucht immer Hilfe, Beistand, um nicht zu fallen.

Ein anderer wie ein Schatten muss ihn immer begleiten.

Mi a határtalan boldogság?

Határtalan boldogság az, ha valaki megéri a nyolcvanat?

De hiszen egy aggastyánra nem vár más csak a magány.

Egy élemedett embert, duplává tesz az állandó árny.

"Csak akkor nem esem el, ha valaki állandóan gyámol, ápolgat."

賀輔仁大學法文研究所所長

趙德恕博士（**Dr. Zsoldos**）

六十華誕

輔仁欽博學，

公教仰宏宣；

今日嵩齡慶，

中華結善緣。

To The Very Reverend Imre P. Zsoldos, Dean of Fujen Catholic University's French Graduate School, on his 60th birthday.

For his broad and profound knowledge
Fujen respects him greatly,
For his unsparing dissemination of the doctrine
The Catholics highly congratulate him.
On the auspicious occasion of his 60th birthday,
We wish him the best of health and prosperity.

Félicitations!

Au Révérend Père Imre P.Zsoldos svd,

Directeur de l'Institut de Français

A l'université catholique Fu Jen,

A l'occasion de son 60-ème anniversaire.

Pour sa connaissance profonde et vaste

Fu Jen lui rend hommage et le respecte.

Pour la dissemination infatigable de la vérité

Les catholiques le félicitent de tout coeur.

En ce jour glorieux de son 60-ème anniversaire,

Nous lui souhaitons bonne santé et prosperité.

Dem Hochwürdigen Imre P.Zsoldos svd,

Direktor des Französischen Institutes

Der Fu Jen Catholic University,

Zu seinem 60-sten Geburtstag,

Seiner unfangreichen und tiefen Kenntnisse wegen,

Wird Fu Jen allerobter Respekt entgegengebracht.

Für seine unermüdliche Verbreitung der Warheit

Danken ihm alle Katholiken.

Anlässlich seines 60-sten Geburtstags, halten wir

Für ihn, die bestenWünsche zur guten Gesundheit

Und einem Leben in Zufriedenheit bereit.

Gratuláció

Ft. Zsoldos Imre verbita atyának,

Fuzsen Katolikus Egyetem

Tanszékvezető Tanárának

Szóljon ez az őszinte kivánat

Hatvanadik születésnapjára.

Mély és sokoldalú tudásáért Fuzsen tiszteli

S hódolattal adózik neki.

Az igazság fáradhatatlan hirdetéséért

Sok katolikus hívő szívből köszönti.

Ragyogó 60-ik születése napján

Jó egészséget és sikert kívánunk neki.

颱　風(一)

十級強風百籟喧，
傾盆大雨隔窗聞；
突然停電天昏暗，
大小人家水到門。

Typhoon (I)

Strong wind is roaring from all sides.

Heavy rain-splash can be heard outside the window.

Sudden power failure darkens sky and earth.

Everyone finds the flood coming and rising at the door.

Thyphon (I)

UN VENT FORT HURLE DE TOUS LES CÔTÉS.
UNE PLUIE TORRENTIELLE SE FAIT ENTENDRE
A TRAVERS LES FENÊTRES, UN CIRCUIT FERME
CRÉE DE L'OBSCURITÉ. TOUT LE MONDE
SENT L'EAU INONDER LA MAISON.

Taifun (I)

Ein starker Wind heult von allen Seiten.

Draussen hört man die Fenster seufzen,

wie der Regen sie prügelt. Ein Kurzschluss

macht Schluss mit den Lichtern. Finsterniss

in Himmel und auf Erde. Das Wasser strömt

in das Haus wie es vom Kübel gegossen wäre.

Tifon (I)

Üvölt a szél mindenfelől hangosan
Erős eső veri az ablakokat.
Sötétséget okoz az áramzárlat,
Vizözönre emlékeztet a tifon.

颱　風(二)

十片烏雲十級颱，
漫天暴雨頓成災；
沿途樹木蕭蕭下，
遍地洪流滾滾來。
千里傷懷長作客，
一生逃難獨留臺；
他鄉日久故鄉遠，
亂世飄萍不盡哀！

Typhoon (II)

Dreadfully strong winds sweep the sky covered with dark clouds.

Storms are ruthless, leaving ruins and corpses in their course.

Trees are bare of branches and leaves fallen in desolation.

Torrents can be seen running from all sides.

A lonely heart, thousands miles away comes up with deep sorrow.

Seeking refuge from war, living alone in Taiwan.

Long time in a strange land, makes one feel the home country far away.

Grief for moving about like duckweed in anarchy is endless.

Thyphon (Ⅱ)

Des vents terriblement forts apportent des nuées noires au ciel

L'orage est si cruel; il ne laisse que ruines et cadavres à son passage.

Les arbres sont denudés, sans feuilles, sans branches.

Les eaux pluviales battent de tous les côtés.

Un refugié venu du continent en souffre encore plus:

Là, c'était la guerre; ici, c'est la solitude et la misère.

De longues années loin de son pays natal

Rendent la vie dure à supporter, rebarbarative, brutale.

Taifun (II)

Der schwarze Himmel wird vom schrecklichen Wind durchgefegt. Unmenschliche Stürme lassen nur Ruinen und Leiche hinter sich. Die Bäume sind nackt, ohne Blätter, ohne Zweigen. (Man sieht den Himmel gar nicht voll mit Geigen!) Wasser überall und Überschwemmungen: für einen Festländer von China ist es noch unerträglicher als für die Anderen, die hier geboren sind. Wenn man leidet, das Gefühl der Heimatlosigkeit wiegt noch schwerer. Hoffentlich wird das keine endlose Anarchie kreieren.

Tifon (𝕀)

Sötét az ég, majd mindonhol beborult.
Dúl-fúl a szél, söpör mindent az uton.
Törött ágak, kicsavart fák, sok a holt.
Vizáradat önt el mindent, ez a tifon

A javából! Csak a szegény menekült,
Ki Kínából úgy ahogy ide jutott,
Szenved, pedig arcán a honvágy kiült.
Jó, hogy ez nem anarchiába fúlt!

颱　　風㈢

新聞廣播有強颱，
十級狂風挾雨來；
路上樹枝多折斷，
菲台琉日算天災。

Typhoon (III)

A strong typhoon is reported in newspapers and broadcast.

Fierce wind with rain sweeps across the country.

Many trees and branches along the streets are broken.

Philippines, Taiwan, Ryuku and Japan share the same calamity.

Thyphon (|||)

Les radios et les journaux annoncent un thyphon

Qui veut s'abbattre avec toute sa force sur le pays:

Branches cassées, arbres tordus le long des chemins:

Les Philippines, Taiwan, Okinava, Japan ont été tous touchés.

TAIFUN (|||)

In den Zeitungen und Radionanmeldungen ist ein 'Taitun angekündigt. Hässliche Windstürme heulen am Lande. Bäume and Äste legen im Wirrwarr in einer Menge. Die Philippinen, Taiwan, Okinava, Japan, alle haben die gleiche Kalamität erlitten.

TIFON (|||)

Újság, rádió röppenti a rossz hírt,
hogy jön a tifon és mindent eláraszt.
Szél zúg, eső hull, kitört fák, holtak,
katasztrófa. Japan, Tajvan, Okinava sírt.

贈 **Dr. Zsoldos**

臺北相逢開會時，

知交五載又分離；

別兄何物堪持贈，

紙短情長一首詩。

其　二

與兄相處是機緣，

詩會同吟又共筵；

今日君家東歐返，

教書報國亦神仙。

To Dr. Imre P. Zsoldos

I

We met in Taipei during a conference.

We said Good-bye, but it was five years of friendship that followed.

I wondered what kind of gift could I present to him:

A verse may reveal my deep feeling, better than anything.

II

It is a chance and opportunity to be in company with you.

We enjoyed the same feast when poems were sung at gatherings.

You are going to return home to Eastern Europe today.

What a pleasure will it be for you to teach in your homeland !

A Dr. Imre P. ZSOLDOS

I

Nous nous vîmes à Taïpei pendant une conférence;

Et puis nous dîmes adieu après qu'elle fut terminée.

Pourtant une amitié de cinq ans s'en est suivie.

Je me suis demandé quel cadeau pourrais-je t'offrir

Et je trouvais qu'un pòeme pourrait le mieux exprimer

Mon estime profond et sincere pour toi.

II

C'est une chance et une unique occasion d'être dans ta companie.

Nous nous sommes réjouis en lisant, en chantant des poèmes

Pendant notre congrès. Aujourd'hui, tu rentres à l'Europe Est,

ton pays natal. Quelle joie sera pour toi d'y enseigner!

An Dr. Imre Zsoldos

I

Wir haben uns in Taipei getroffen während eines Kongresses.

Nach dem Kongress haben wir einander Ade gewinkt,

Aber eine fünfjährige Freundschaft ist unter uns entstanden.

Ich fragte mich was für ein Geschänk ich dir zum Abschied geben könnte ? Ein Gedicht, glaube ich, wäre das Beste, um meine aufrichtige Gefühle zum Ausdruck zu bringen.

II

Es ist eine Chance und gute Gelegenheit in deiner Kompanie zu sein.

Wir haben am gleichen Kongress unsere Gedichte gelesen, gesungen.

Heute kehrst du zur Osteurope, zu deinem Heimatland zuruck. Was für eine Freude wird es für Dich sein, dort unterrichten zu dürfen!

Dr. Zsoldos Imrenek

Taipeben találkoztunk egy konferencián.
Búcsút mondtunk akkor, de búcsúnkat
Öt év barátság követte.
Kérdezgettem milyen adjándékot tudnék neked adni.
Ekkor született meg bennem e költemény,
Amely legjobban kifejezi mély érzéseimet.

Öröm, egy sansz, ha társaságodban lehetek.
Együtt örültünk a költemények olvasásának,
Éneklésének összejöveteleinkkor.
Ma Kelet-Europába mész, visszatérsz hazádba...
Mily öröm, hogy most otthon taníthatsz!

白衣天使

一調寄南柯子一

一臉溫柔相
輕盈天使裝
玉人含笑來而往
儀態端莊
親切似冬陽

微笑輕聲說
慇懃問暖涼
上班總爲病人忙
慈善心腸
贏得美名揚

The Nurse

Dressed up in tenderness

Joyous and ange-like

Fair lady, comes and goes smilingly

Polite and courteous

Warm as the winter sun,

Speaking with your smile

Asking kindly after the patient's health

Fully dedicated to them

Kind and charitable

You earn fame and respect.

L'INFIRMIERE

VÊTUE EN TENDRESSE

HEUREUSE COMME UN ANGE

ELLE VA ET VIENT EN SOURIANT:

POLIE ET COURTOISE

ELLE NOUS RECHAUFFE

COMME LE SOLEIL EN HIVER.

SON SOURIRE EST SA PAROLE

LOSQU'ELLE DEMANDE AUX PATIENTS

LEUR ÉTAT DE SANTÉ.

ELLE EST ENTIÈREMENT DÉVOUÉE À EUX,

CHARITABLE ET TENDRE,

ELLE MÉRITE TOUS NOS RESPECTS ET LOUANGES.

Die Krankepflägerin

Gekleidet in Zartheit

Froh wie ein Engel,

Sie geht ein und aus

Von Zimmer zu Zimmer,

Lächelnd, höflich.

Eine echte Sonne im Winter.

Ihre Sprache ist ihr Lächeln.

Liebend fragt den Patienten

Nach seinem Zustand.

Sie gibt ihnen ihr ganzes Leben.

Hilfsbereit und ergeben.

Dank und Ehre seien ihr dafür gegeben!

A nővérke

Gyöngédség a ruhája,

Igaz, kedves angyalka.

Mosolyogva jár-kel.

Csiszolt a modora, finom.

Hideg télben meleg napom.

Mosolyával beszél,

Kérdezi a beteget,

Hogy aludt, hogy evett?

Szolgálata odaadó, teljes,

Szeretetben díjnyertes.

Hála neki s tisztelet!

傳　情

芳心原欲訴，
見面卻無言；
柳眼傳深意，
蒙君一笑溫。

Communication of Love

Her heart should have been revealed earlier.

But no words were uttered when met.

Attractive eyes communicated real affection.

A smile in response warmed up what she felt.

Communication de l'amour

Son coeur aurait du se révèler plus tôt
Mais à notre rencontre on n'a dit un seul mot:
Ses yeux attirants parlaient d'une affection réelle,
Son sourire fut une chaude réponse et dit ce qui était elle.

Mitteilung der Liebe

Ihr Herz hätte schon lange her irgendein Zeichen gegeben,

Wir sagten aber nichts zu einandern, wenn wir uns begegneten.

Ihre reizenden Augen sprachen von einer echten Liebe.

Ein Lächeln war genügende Antwort für mich über ihre Gefühle.

Szeretetközlés

Már régesrég megmutathatta volna a szívét,

De némák maradtunk, amikor egymást megláttuk.

Szép szemében fejezte ki szive igaz érzelmet,

Hogy szeretett, annak mosolya adta a jelét.

生與死

來如流水去如風，
恍若人生一夢中；
不得不流流入世，
飄飄逝去亦無蹤。

Birth and Death

It comes like a flow and vanishes like a wind.

Lifetime for human beings seems to be a dream.

Flowing to the world by force without its own will.

But disappearing also like a leaving wind never to return.

VIE ET MORT

Elle vient comme le courant et disparaît comme le vent.

L'existence humaine n'est qu'un rêve,- en apparence.

On ne nous pose aucune question sur notre naissance.

Et on ne demande pas non plus si voulons ou non la partance.

LEBEN UND TOD

Es kommt wie der Strom und verschwindet wie der Wind.

Scheinbar ist das menschliche Leben nichts anders als ein Traum.

Man wird nie gefragt weder über sein eigenes Sein noch über seinen Tod.

Aber ein nimmer zurückkehrender Wind ist der Abschied vom Leben.

ÉLET ÉS HALÁL

Jön mint az áramlat és elillan mint a szél.

Életünk, - látszólag - nem más mint egy álom.

Nem vár választ tőlunk igent vagy nemet senki a létre.

Távozásod vedd úgy, hogy visszanemtérő szél lett belőle.

榮總清晨

樂得生平清早閒，
院前散步不同凡；
既無來往人車擠，
復可逍遙路樹間。

Early Morning in Veterans General Hospital

Glad to take a walk leisurely.

In the unusual front yard in the early morning.

No pedestrians, nor vehicles to bother.

It is so enjoyable to loiter under the roadside trees.

Dans l'hôpital des vétérans

Je suis content de me promener de bonne heure

Dans le jardin habituel des vétérans devant l'hôpital:

Pas de piétons, pas de motos qui me dérangeraient.

C'est tellement agréable, à faire sa ronde sous les

arbres le long du trottoir.

In dem Spital der Veteraner

Ich freue mich über das ungenierte Spazieren

in dem gewohnten Park des Spitals der Veteraner.

Kein Fussgänger, keine Fahrzeuge, die mich genierten.

Es ist so angenehm, unter den Bäumen, entlang des

Trottoirs herumzuspazieren.

Kora reggel a vétéránok közkórházában

Örömmel tölt el ez a korareggeli szabad séta
A közkórház előtti megszokott parkban.

Nem háborgatnak sem gyalogosok, sem járművek.

Kellemes a járda melletti fák alatt a bandukolás.

重　逢

日日思君心事重，
朝朝盼望再相逢；
席間人雜情難訴，
微笑點頭意已通。

Meet Again

I miss you day after day with deep worry.

I never cease to hope to meet you again.

I could not tell all I had in mind before the party.

A smiling nod at each other was enough to communicate.

Nouvelle rencontre

Tu me manques chaque jour et je m'en soucie.

Je ne cesse quand même d'espérer te revoir.

Je ne pouvais pas te dire ce que je te voulais à la partie.

Une inclination de tête souriante mutuelle nous suffit.

Neue Begegnung

Ich habe dich sehr vermisst und ich hab' Kummer,

Ich höre doch nicht auf zu hoffen, dass wir uns eines

Tages treffen werden.

Ich könnte dir nicht sagen, was ich sagen wollte während

der Partie.

Ein lächelneds Kopfbewegen reichte uns, um es mitzuteilen.

Újratalálkozás

Mély aggódással gondolok rád nap mint nap.

Csupán az éltet, hogy újra találkozunk.

A partin azonban ajkam szótlan marad,

Elég az, hogy csendben egymásra mosolygunk.

眞　情

笑裡低聲語，
相看無限情；
甜言猶在耳，
舉止露眞誠。

Deep affection

A smile is kept at all times in subdued contour.

Frequent gaze seems to show unlimited emotion.

Honey words seem to be heard still in the ears.

The deportment and behavior reveal her deep affection.

Affection profonde

Un sourire doit être toujours adouci:

Un clin d'oeil fréquent est signe de passion incontrôlée:

Les doux mots d'amour resonnent longtemps dans les oreilles:

Belle conduite et civilité manifestent une affection profonde.

Tiefe Gefühle

Ein Lächeln muss immer gemildert werden.

Ein häufiger Blick ist immer Zeichen unbändiger Gefühle.

Worte der Liebe werden lange in den Ohren resonieren.

Das Verhalter und das Benehmen einer Person

manifestieren immer ein tiefes Gefühl.

Hogy mély maradjon a szeretet...

A mosolyt visszafojtottsággal kell folyton vedenünk,

Hogy a szép szavakat sokáig visszhangozza fülünk.

Ha úgy tünik végtelen érzelmek tükre a szemünk,

Mély szeretetről tanúskodjék mindenegyes tettünk.

老詩人吟

早知人必死，

來日剩無多；

定靜除焦慮，

吟詩鬥病魔。

Old Poet

I know everyone must die some time.

There is less time to leave us now.

I have to be calm and get rid of anxiety.

I must chant poems against the devil of ill.

Vieux poète

Je sais qu'un jour tout le monde doit mourir.

Nous n'avons pas beaucoup de temps même si la vie est longue.

Je dois être calme et ne m'en soucier pas trop.

Je dois chanter mes poèmes pour guérir ces maux.

Alter Dichter

Ich weiss, dass wir eines Tages alle sterbon müssen:

Wir haben nicht viel Zeit, auch wenn wir lange leben.

Ich muss ruhig sein und mich nicht zu viel kümmern.

Ich muss meine Gedichte singen, um den Teufel dieses

Quales zu vertreiben.

Öreg költő

Tudom, hogy egy napon mindenkinek meg kell halnia,

S ha hosszú is az élet, az időből sosem fútja.

Nyugalom a fontos tehát, nem szabad bánkodni.

Ezért éneklem én a költemenyeimet, hátha sikerül

majd ezt az ördögöt megszalasztani.

單　戀

年華空度過，
花燭了無期；
整日徒長嘆，
含情欲告誰？

其二

和風吹翠葉，
閒坐荷池傍；
不負相思意，
遙看狄克楊。

Unilateral Love

I

Days of a youngster are spent in futility.

Time for wedding can be remote.

Long sigh continues day after day.

(He does not know when the wedding

can be expected.)

To whom his love should be disclosed!

II

Gentle wind blows on green leaves.

A little rest beside the lotus pond.

In response to deep friendly sentiments.

Take a remote look at Dick Young.

Amour unilateral

I

Les jeunes gens mènent une vie futile;

Plus ils se marient tard mieux cela vaut.

Les longs jours se passent en soupirs.

(Ils ne savent pas exactement quand

le mariage devrait avoir lieu.)

Ils ne savent pas qui devraient-ils aimer!

II

Une brise douce souffle sur les feuilles vertes.

Je peux m'assoir à côté de l'étang des nénuphars

Pour passer un peu de temps avec un ami venu

me voir. L'amitie entre lui est moi s'est fait valoir.

Einseitige Liebe

I

Junge Leute treiben nur Unsinn.

Sie können ruhig mit dem Heiraten warten.

Jeder Tag ist nachher mit Seufzen verbracht.

(Sie wissen nicht genau, wenn sie eigentlich
  heiraten müssten!)

Sie wissen auch nicht wie sie lieben sollten.

II

Eine sanfte Brise weht durch die grünen Ästen.

Ich setze mich hin neben dem Lotusteich,

um mich ein bischen auszuruhen mit einem Freund, der kam,

um mich zu besuchen. Unsere Freundschaft hat sich sicherlich

verdient gemacht.

Egyoldalú szertetet

I

A fiatalok ostobaságokkal töltik el éveiket.

Többet kellene a házasodással várniok.

Utána nem más mint sopánkodás vár csak rájuk.

(Nem tudják pontosan, hogy mi a legjobb kor a házasságra.)

S azt sem tudják igazában, hogy mi a szeretet.

II

Enyhe szellő fújja a zöld leveleket.

Leülok a padra a lótusztó mellett.

A barátommal, aki látogatni jött engemet.

Ez a barátság már bebizonyosultan igazi szereretet.

附錄
APPENDIX

Boundless Bliss?

Is it boundless bliss when one lives till
eight'y?
But an old man must always face sour
solitude.
He must be taken care of to prevent
stumbling,
Two men have to back him up when
he is so ageing

Deep Affection

A smile is kept at all times in subdued
contour.
A frequent gaze seems to show
unlimited emotion.
Honey-words seem to be heard still in
the ears.
The deportment and behavior reveal her
deep affection.

Dr. Hsu, Shih-Tze (徐世澤)
(Stephen Shih-tze, HSU)

1427-2F, VGH East District
Shih-Pai Road, Section 2
Peitou, Taipei, Taiwan, R.O.C.
Tel: 886-2-871-3250

March 13, 1929

Medical doctor
Editor-in-chief, N.D.M.C. Monthly
(National Defense Medical Center)
Secretary chief, Chinese Poets
    Association in Taipei, Taiwan

Communication of Love

Her heart should have been revealed
earlier.
But no words were uttered when met.
Attractive eyes communicated real
affection.
A smile in response warmed up what
she felt.

Meet Again

I miss you day after day with deep
worry.
I never cease to hope to meet you
again.
I could not tell all I had in mind before
the party.
A smiling nod at each other was
enough to communicate.

The Falcon Rose

It rises

In my sight

A russet moon

From my Frozen banks

Geese

Fly to the meres of the sky

A red sun

Bathes in my lake

My Thunder Bird

Sees deep in the night of the
  hawkweeds

And the moose of my desires

Bells in the vast hairy savannas

Of my red clay memory

La Rose épervière

Il se lève

En mon cristallin

Une lune rousse

De mes rivages gelés

Des outardes

Volent aux mares du ciel

Un soleil rouge

Se baigne dans mon lac

Mon Oiseau-Tonnerre

Voit, profond dans la nuit des
  épervières

Et l'orignal de mes désirs

Brame dans les vastes savanes
  chevelues

De ma mémoire de glaise rouge.

Prof. Evelyne Anne Voldeng

French Department
Carleton University
1125 Colonel By Drive
Ottawa, Ontario, K1S 5B6, Canada
Tel: 1-613-520-2194 (O)
    1-613-257-4290 (H)
Fax: 1-613-520-3544

Born in Brittany in 1943

Publication:
Tessons
Le Journal des poètes
Fireweed
Les Femmes et les mots
Envol

Après une étude de la nature dans la
poésie de John Keats, elle s'est
intéressée à l'œuvre de Tristan
Corbière, puis aux écritures féminines

The Year 2097.
A Cosmomessage
from the Bard-Earthologist from the
spaceship "IloveU" to for the President of
the 17th World Congress of Poets,
Seoul-1997, Dr. Han-Yi Baek

There is no concept of being "provincial"
In the boundless universe, bespangled
With planets inhabited by thinking life
　　　　　forms.
Thinking creatures cannot be confined
By any fence, wall, or boundary. No
　　　　　borders
Can separate spiritual siblings. And
　　　　　whatever
Part of the limitless space is enriched
　　　　　by thoughts
Of a human or another sapient being –
　　That is the capital of capitals.

For instance, who would have ever
　　　　　thought,
Brothers, that it would be in Seoul,
Of all places, where we would pledge
Our allegiance to both past and future
Ideals of intergalactic brotherhood,
There, where the World Congress of Poets
Solidifies the essence of spirituality
　　　　Into golden poems.

Translated from Cosmospheranto

The 17th World Congress of Poets.
August 1997. Seoul, Korea.

We enrich our days and years,
And, seing stars, long for height.

Strengthen thy, o Poetry, successes:
Impulses, energy, ideas!

Мы дни /Поэзия борьбы
и годы　　крепи свои
делаем　　　удачи
богаче　　　живая
и видя　　　кровь
звезды　　　порыв
жаждем　　полет
Theвысоты　мечты Th

Mr. Viktor A. Ourin

Olympoetry Movement
3395 Neptune Ave. 124
Brooklyn , New York 11224, USA
Tel: 1-718-373-0719

Founder and president
Olympoetry Movement

Nature Modern Living

Here in California foothills where scene
is green
　and the streams flow full from
　　mountain snow
　while springtime blossoms into
　　pink, white, yellow

we feel a call to come away from it all,
　to leave the concrete and close
　　buildings tall
　　to stretch our arms and breathe in
　　scented nature

to touch closely our lonely, into
　withdrawn calm
　from fast-lane living, our
　　programmed lives,
　　trying to capture respite solitaire,
　　rewarding

then encapsule it to take back
tomorrow
　remembering to resolve to do it often,
　again,
　　so when over-scheduled, take time
　　out, uncover

the within, buried, to draw on when
tense
　or stressed, gently using nature to
　calm us,
　　drawing new spiritual solace,
　　happiness,
　　for modern living and nature do
　　complement us:

See it, feel it, paint it, poetry it, set it
　to music
For here is 'lyrical faith in God, love of
　beauty of His works.'*

* Robert Southwell, S.J. 1561-1595
　England

Dr. Rosemary C. Wilkinson

3146 Buckeye Court
Placerville, CA 95667, U.S.A.
Tel: 1-916-626-4166
Fax: 1-916-642-2183

February 21

President of World Congress of Poets,
　World Academy of Arts and Culture

Publication:
Grosart-1972 best edition of his works
　(Robert Southwell, S.J.)
Hood's-1926 The Book of Robert Southwell
Janelle-1935 The Writer
Christopher Devlin-1955 The Easton
　Press, Norwalk, CT, U.S.A.

Anthology of Natural Modernism
World Poets

Author : World Poets & Han-Yi Baek
Published by : Han Midia Co., Ltd.

Published : August 1997.
Printed : August 1997.
ISBN 89-7762-044-9

ISBN 89-7762-044-9
03810
9 788977 620445

A STUDY OF THE TANG POETRY

by Stephen Shihtze Hsu

What is poetry?

A good definition would be : an arrangement of words that aims at achieving an imaginative awareness of an experience by creating a specific emotional response. Its words aim not only at meanings and ideas, but also at sounds and rhythms. Occasionally, it also creates colorful images.

While being sick or having troubles, some people like to take with them a copy of poems to read and recite, so that they can feel calm and relaxed. Reading or humming a stanza is a kind of recreation. One of the most effective means of elevating one's mind is the reading Tang poetry.

Poetry is lyrical, and as such, it has a direct appeal to emotion. Since it is rhythmical, it has direct appeal to feeling, and music.

For this reason when we read a stanza of poetry, it is natural and easy for us to calm down and relax. There is an old saying that poetry can cultivate a human being's disposition. The famous dictum is certified to be true because of the poet's gentleness, sincerity and honesty. A poet needs to control his own emotions, for only while he is in a calm mood, can he think of how to make comprehensive and proper verses. Only poems made by a poet at such a time can be appreciated by people. A poet has a sentiment, he gives much thought to the feelings of other people, and so when we recite his poem we feel that it is a beautiful work of literature.

The Tang Dynasty was a poetic time, because officials were selected on the basis of an examination in poetry. Poetry was not only used as a method of examination, but also as a song.

Therefore, at that time many great poets appeared, and different poetic styles were developed. The Chinese are never tired of Tang poetry, of which the most famous verses are as familiar in Asia as Shakespeare's in the English-speaking world. The poetry of the Tang Dynasty (A. D. 618-907) consisting of 48,900 poems (3.3 million Chinese characters) by 2,200 poets, can provide a wealth to Chinese culture.

Tang poets were particularly fond of writing about the moon, the wind, the clouds and mountains, as each of those Chinese characters appears for more than 12,000 times in their poems.

The character for wine appears only 5,762 times, even though drinking was a favorite topic and evocation of "Fairy" Poet Li Pai (A. D. 702-762). He was perhaps the greatest poet of that era. He wrote : "0, what infinite charms I find in wine ! ".

The Sage Poet Tu Fu (A. D. 712-770) wrote in "My Trip from the Capital to Fengyi Hsiang". "Inside the vermilion gate wine and meat are stinking; On the roadside lie the bones of people frozen to death".

Everyone should read the selection of these poems. One of the best and the most famous selection of poems is that of three hundred pieces of Tang poetry which have proven peerless throughout the ages. In fact, this selection of poems consists of 310 poems selected from 77 poets.

Therefore, the selection of poems is reduced to 310 pieces of Tang poems. These poems are generally recognized as the best. Until now it was very common for people to learn, study and imitate Tang poems. There are a few foreign language translations of Tang poems. The poems not only can be hummed and appreciated, but can also cultivate the character. There is an old saying that having well read 300 pieces of Tang poetry, a man who could not hum formerly can hum now. This means that to read Tang poetry well is really to recite the poems with appreciation.

There are six types of Tang poems : the classical poems of five characters in a line, the classical poems of seven characters in a line, a quatrain with five characters in each line, ottava rima with five characters in each line, a quatrain with seven characters in each line and ottava rima with seven characters in each line. They are classified according to the number of characters, rhythm (tone) and verbal parallelism. The rhythm of a poem is regular and based on the tones of the words. The four (or five) tones of words are : level tone, high-level tone, rising tone, falling-rising tone and falling tone. The former two are called "level" tones and the latter "oblique" tones. In addition, there is an entering tone emerged from an oblique tone. One who doesn't understand level tones and oblique tones can observe the repetition of the symmetry of a poem. The ottava rima with five or seven characters each is composed of two groups of rhythm which are repeated and uniform.

When we read silently a poem of chant level and oblique tones, we will naturally feel that it is read smoothly, pleasing to the ears. One can enjoy the change of tones just like a man, listening to Chinese opera, can distinguish good and bad singing although he doesn't understand the rest of the opera.

Allusion and ambiguity are pervasive features in Chinese poetry and their strength is derived from the effective use of metaphor. Metaphor is generally rooted in the commonplace and is universal in its comprehensibility. The primary function of metaphor and allusion is to heighten the emotional tenor of a poem. To do so, metaphors must be concise and pithy. While novelty is important, this should not be at the expense of coherence. Historical allusions are among the most common in the Chinese tradition.

Brevity and succinct expression lie at the heart of poetry, far more so than in prose. Four-line verses in particular must achieve verbal economy without compromising a natural feeling.

Seven-character quatrains are generally composed for singing. They must be concise and pithy, yet easily understood. The arts of music and painting were highly advanced in the Tang and their interrelationship with poetry was a key factor in the development of all three arts.

The reader of Tang poetry must identify with the Tang literary aesthetic and view its poetry in that context. But in addition, the works should serve to enlighten us, in any circumstance, much as do the reading of philosophy or history. By applying leisure time to recitation of the classics, one can rectify one's character and ennoble one's thoughts.

I believe that poetry must be accessible to all people, in all places and all walks of life. I am a physician residing in the Republic of China. I compose poetry in common and modern terms, without recourse to the archaic or the obscurantist. Others may still write in the style of the ancients, employing clever allusions and historical references. My works, however, represent a more modern aesthetic which, I hope, future generations will respect as appropriate to our modern circumstances and tastes.

Now I introduce the following pieces of poems I wrote in six different styles：

1. Wuu Jyuer（五絶）：quatrain in five characters in each line. A poem in four lines, five-characters each. Such as："To the Very Reverend Imre P. Zsoldos" and "Deep Affection".

2. Chi Jyuer（七絶）：quatrain in seven characters in each line. A poem in four lines, seven-characters each. Such as："Welcome-rain in Tucson" and "The New York Subway".

3. Wuu lyuh（五律）：Ottava rima in five characters in each line. A prescribed verse, eight lines, five characters each such as："Welcome to Overseas Poets' Participation in Taipei's World Congress".

4. Chi lyuh（七律）：Ottava rima in seven characters in each line. A prescribed verse, eight lines, seven characters each. Such as；"Regimen".

5. Tsyr（詞）：In varied tonal patterns and sentence lengths. Such as："The Nurse" and "A Prominent Poet".

6. New poetry（現代詩）：New poetry in contrast with the classical one. Such as："Walking stick" and "Defence of Cancer".

Note：

1. Level＝Even＝Ping(平)
2. Oblique＝Ze(仄)

Taipei, May 20, 1993　　　　　　Hsu Shih-Tze D. D. S., M. P. H.

作者小傳

　　徐世澤　江蘇東台（興化）人，一九二九年三月十三日生。國防醫學院醫學士、公共衛生學碩士。曾赴美、澳、紐等國考察研究，數度代表出席世界詩人大會，足跡遍六大洲五十五國。曾任主任、秘書、副院長、院長、榮總人月刊總編輯等。作品散見各報章雜誌及列入世界詩人選集，出版中英對照「養生吟」詩集，曾榮獲教育部詩教獎。現任中國詩經研究會秘書長、乾坤詩刊社副社長、源遠月刊編輯等。

"Poetry is the record of the best and happiest moments of the happiest and best minds" Percy Bysshe SHELLEY

We congratulate Dr. HSU for the best poems of his best mind with the quotation above.

VIKTOR OURIN, OLYMPOETRY,FOUNDER,PRESIDENT

Dr. FRANK BUDENHOLZER,SVD,FUJEN UNIVERSITY, VICE PRESIDENT

Dr. JAC KUEPERS,SVD,CHINA PROVINCE,PROVINCIAL

DDr. GYULA Molnár,HUNGARY, AUTHOR

Br. PAT HOGAN SVD.MA. FUJEN UNIVERSITY,MANDARIN CENTER,DIRECTOR

Dr. IMRE ZSOLDOS, SVD. FUJEN UNIVERSITY,PROFESSOR

Introduction of Dr. Hsu Shih-tze

DR. HSU SHIH-TZE (Stephen Shih-Tze HSU) was born on March 13, 1929. Now he lives at the Peitou district, Taipei, Taiwan. His native home was Hsucheng village, in the northern Kiangsu. After he gradua-ted from the National Defense Medical Center, and had obtained the degree of D.D.S. and that of the M.P.H. he assumed the positions of physician in charge, section chief, deputy director and hospital director etc. In 1967, he went to Australia and New Zealand to study the systems of Medical Care there. In 1982 and in 1985, he went to the USA to visit seven Veterans Medical Centers. At present, he is editor-in-chief of the " N.D.M.C. Monthly", deputy director of the "Chien Kun Poetry Quar-terly" and secretary-in-chief to the Chinese Poets Association in Taipei, Taiwan. He has been traveling in 55 countries. He has received many awards, among others, one in 1992, from the Ministry of Education. **REGIMEN**, the anthology of his poems from which this selection was made, was published in 1994.

Address:

Dr. Hsu Shih-Tze

147-2 Fl. VGH East District

Shih-Pai Road, Sec.2.

PEITOU, TAIPEI, TAIWAN, ROC.

Tel.: (02) 2871-3250

Biographie

DR.HSU SHIH-TZE (Etienne Shih-Tze HSU) est né le 13 mars 1929. A présent, il habite dans la banlieu de Taïpeîh, à Peitou, Taiwan. Son pays natal est le village Hsucheng, au nord de Kansu. Après être diplomé en médicine dans le Centre Médical de la Défense, il s'est chargé de toute sorte de postes comme médecin: simple médecin, médecin de la section, sous-directeur de l'hôpital, directeur etc. En 1967 il est allé en Australie et en Nouvelle Zéland pour étudier leur système de soigner les malades. En 1982 et de nouveau en 1985, il est allé aux USA pour visiter sept centres médicaux des vétérans. En ce moment, il est ré dacteur-en-chef d'une revue mensuelle, intitulée NDMC et vice rédecteur-en-chef d'une revue poétique nommée Poésie Chien Kun qui paraît quatre fois par an et, il est sécrétaire général d'une Association Poétique. Il a reçu plusieurs prix à mentionner le Prix du Ministre de l'Education en 1994. Son anthologie de poèmes intitulée REGIMEN dont on a fait la sélection, a été publiée en 1992. Il aime beaucoup voyager et durant ces voyages, il a déjà visité 55 pays.

Adresse:

Dr. HSU SHIH-TZE

147-2 Fl. VGH East District

Shih-Pai Road, Sec.2.

PEITOU, TAIPEI, TAIWAN, ROC.

Tel.: (02) 2871-3250

Biographie

Dr. HSU SHIH-TZE (Stefan Shih-Tze HSU) ist am 13ten März 1929 geboren. Zur Zeit lebt er in der Peripherie von Taipei, in Peitou. Seine Geburtsort war das Dorf Hsucheng, im Nord von Kansu. Nachdem er sein Doktor in Modizin in dem Zentrum der Nazionalen Verteidigung gemacht hat, hat er in verschiedenen Posten als Artzt praktiziert, zuerst mal als gewöhnlicher Arzt und später als Assistent Direktor des Spitals und auch als Direktor etc. Im Jahre 1967 ist er nach Australien und Zach Neu-Zeland gegangen, um dort die Systeme der ärtzlichen Behandlungen,zu studieren. Im Jahre 1982 und wieder einmal im Jahre 1985 ist er nach der USA gereist,um dort sieben Medizinische Zentrums der Veteraner zu besichtigen. Zur Zeit ist er Chef-Redaktor einer monatlichen Zeitschrift, die NDMC heisst, und also Assistent Direktor einer dichterischen Zeitschrift, die viermal im Jahre publiziert wird. Ausserdem ist er auch General-Sekräter einer Chinesischen Poetischen Versammlung. Er hat mehrere Preise für seine Dichtungen bekommen, unten denen der höchstwertvolle von dem Erziehungsminister von Taiwan, im Jahre 1992. Die ausgewähteln Gedichte, die wir in diesem Buch publizieren, sind in der Anthologie REGIMEN im Jahre 1994 erschienen worden. Dr. Hsu reist sehr viel, er hat schon 55 Länder besichtigt.

Seine Adresse:

Dr. HSU Shih-Tze

147-2 Fl. VGH East District

Shih-Pai Road, Sec.2.

PEITOU, Taipei, Taiwan, ROC.

Tel.: (02) 2871-3250

Dr.Hsu életrajza

Dr. HSU-SHIH-TZE (Hsu Shih-Tze István) 1929 március 13án született. Jelenleg Tajvanban, Taipei külvárosában, Peitouban él. Szülő falúja Hsucheng, az észak Kanszu tartományban van.

Miután a Honvédelmi Minisztérium Orvostudományi Egyetemén diplomát szerzett, többféle beosztásban működött: kezdet-kezdetén mint cselédkönyves orvos, utána mint csoportvezető orvos, igazgató helyettes, igazgató stb. 1967-ben Ausztráliában és Új-Zélandban az ottani orvosi ellátást tanulmányozta. 1982-ben és 1985-ben USA-ban végzett látogatást hét katona-kórházban. Jelenleg az NDMC havi folyóirat igazgatójaként működik és a Chien Kun Költők négyhavonként megjelenő folyóirat helyettes igazgatója. A tajvani Költők Társaságának főtitkári tisztségét is betölti Taipeiben. Sokat utazott, 55 országba látogatott el, és tartozkodott ott hosszabb-rövidebb ideig. Sok kitüntetést kapott, a legemlitésre méltóbbat, a Kínai Nevelésügyi Minisztertől 1992-ben. Az Életrend cimű antológiája, amelyből ezeket a költeményeket válogattuk, 1991-ben jelent meg.

Cím:

Dr. HSU Shih-Tze

147-2 em. VGH East District

Shih-Pai Road, Sec.2.

PEITOU, Taipei, Taiwan, ROC.

Tél.: (02) 2871-3250

教育部獎狀

徐世澤先生，致力
推行中華文化，宏
揚詩教有功，特頒
獎狀，用資表彰。

部長　郭為藩

Dr. Hsu receiving the award of the Ministry of Education

Rev. Dr. Imre P. Zsoldos, Mr. Viktor Ourin, Dr. Hsu

Professor Angelo Marenzi and his wife, Dr. Imre Zsoldos, Dr. Hsu

"Poetry is the record of the best and happiest moments of the happiest and best minds". Percy Bysshe Shelley

We congratulate you Dr. Hsu for the selection of your best poems with the quotation above knowing that this thought is very true as far as your poems are also concerned.

Victor Ourin, Olympoetry, Founder, President
Dr. Frank Budenholzer, svd, Fujen University, Vice President
Dr. Jac Kuepers, svd, China Province, Provincial
DDr. Gyula Molnar, Hungary, Author
Mr. and Mrs. Rudolf Szamos, Hungary, Author, Poet, Publisher
Br. Pat Hogan MA, Fujen University, Mandarin Center, Director
Dr. Imre Prince Zsoldos svd, Fujen University, French Department and Graduate School,
Founder, Professor, Poet, Author, Writer, Linguist

Dr. Hsu at the World Congress of Poets in Korea

Dr. Hsu and Dr. Zsoldos receiving the Olympoetry Torch and Award

Dr. Hsu in Argentina

Dr. Hsu and his wife Mrs Hsu in Good Hope Cape

Dr. Hsu in Norway at the North Pole

Dr. Hsu in Greece, country of the First Olympics

Dr. Hsu in Rome, in front of Saint Peter's Cathedral

Dr. Hsu in Amsterdam in front of the Van Gogh Museum

Dr. Hsu in Budapest, on the
Plaza of the Hungarian Heroes

Dr. Hsu
in the Tagore Park near
Lake Balaton in Balatonfüred

後記及感謝語

　　本詩集幸蒙Dr. Imre P.Zsoldos之校訂，韓校長韶華賜序，內子全秀華女士之核稿。并蒙Dr.Randy M.Green, Ms.Shannon Hsu、徐國旺等之協助。使內容精形，編排新穎，更具可讀性。特在此一併致謝。

徐世澤

Postscript

Dr. Hsu Shih-Tse is not only a reputed physician but also a well versed author in poetry. His poems are really of rare beauty and of deep feelings. His verses can be often found in the magazines of VGH Man Monthly and Yuan Yuen Away Sources. His language is modern, plain and simple. Because these poems are rich in emotion and full of meanings, many foreign professors and students in Taiwan like them, especially for his elegant style. Even the director of Cultural Museum across Taiwan Strait in Mainland China has composed verses in response. This shows how deligthed people are at their reading.

A book entitled <u>Regimen</u> was published by Dr. Hsu in July, 1991. It contains his verses both in Chinese and in English. He has sent the books to many poets in 34 countries, aiming at the promotion of Chinese culture.

I am fortunate to have read more than two hundred of Dr. Hsu's verses before they were put into print. I am impressed by the spirit of traditional verses in his writing since they still correspond to the trend of our time. His rich feeling and knowledge reflected in the verses can be hardly forgotten. His book of verses will be reprinted shortly. I am pleased to take the opportunity to write a few words as above for recommendig them in this postscript to the readers who like Chinese verses.

May 6, 1998   Shih Yen-Chang

author

Epilogue

Dr.Hsu Shih-Tse n'est pas seulement un médecin renommé mais aussi un auteur très doué en poésie. Ses poèmes sont vraiment d'une beauté rare et chargés d'émotions. On peut voir ses poèmes dans les magazines comme la mensuelle L'Homme VGH et la Yuan Yuen Away Sources. Sa langue est moderne, claire et simple. Puisque ses poèmes contiennent une richesse d'émotions et de sens profond, beaucoup de professeurs et d'étudiants étrangers à Taiwan les aiment, particulièrement pour leur style élégant. Même le directeur de Musée de la Culture au Continent de Chine a composé des poèmes pour exprimer son appréciation. Ceci montre combien les gens sont contents de les pouvoir lire.

Un recueil entitulé <u>Régime</u> a été publié par Dr. Hsu en 1991. Il contient ses poèmes en deux langues, en chinois et en anglais. Il a envoyé ce receuil de poèmes à de nombreux poètes en 34 pays dans le but de propager la culture chinoise.

J'ai de la chance d'avoir lu plus de 200 de poèmes de Dr.Hsu avant qu'ils soient parus. Je suis impressionné de l'esprit traditionnel que j'ai trouvé dans ces vers puisqu'ils correspondent encore à la vogue de notre temps. Les sentiments et les connaissances profonds reflétés dans ces poèmes, on peut les difficilement oublier. Une séléction de ces poèmes va bientôt paraître. Je suis heureux d'avoir l'occasion de mettre ces quelques mots noir sur blanc en écrivant cet épilogue et en exprimant mes meilleurs voeux à tous les lecteurs qui aiment la poésie chinoise.

le 6 mai, 1998   Shih Yen-Chang

auteur

NACHWORT

Dr. Hsu Shih-Tse ist nicht nur ein berühmter Arzt, sondern auch ein auständiger Dichter. Seine Gedichte sind einer seltenen Schönheit und haben tiefe Gefühle. Seine Dichtungen kann man oft finden in den monatlichen Zeitschriften, in "Der Mann VGH" und "Yuan Yuen Away Quellen". Seie Sprache ist modern, klar und einfach. Weil diese Dichtungen in Gefühlen so reich sind und einen tiefen Sinn haben, sehr viele ausländische Professoren und Studenten lesen sie sehr gern, besoders wegen ihres eleganten Styles. Sogar der Direktor des Kulturmuseums im Festland China hat eine Dichtung geschrieben, um seiner Glückwünsche in diese Art und Weise zum Ausdruck zu bringen. Dies zeigt wie gerne die Leute diese Gedichte lesen.

Ein Buch dessen Titel "Regimen" ist, wurde durch Dr. Hsu im Juli 1991 publiziert. Es enthält seine Gedichte in zwei Sprachen, im Chinesischen und im Eglischen.

Ich bin froh, dass ich mehr als 200 von den Gedichten von Dr. Hsu lesen dürfte, bevor sie im Druck erschienen sind. Ich bin sehr beeindruckt von dem traditionellen Geist dieser Gedichte, weil sie noch der Tendenz der heutigen Zeit korrespondieren. Seine tiefe Gefühle und Kentnisse, die in diesen Gedichten erscheinen, kann man schwer vergessen. Eine gewählte Ausgabe von diesen Gedichten wird bald wieder erscheinen. Ich freue mich riesig, dass ich die Gelegenheit habe, um diese Linien schreiben zu dürfen, damit ich die Lesern, die die chinesischen Gedichte hochschatzen, in diesem Nachwort ermutigen kann.

Den 6ten Mai 1998   Shih Yen-Chang

Autor

Epilógus

Dr. Hsu Shih-Tse nemcsak jóhírű orvos, hanem nagyszerű költő is. Költemenyei valóban ritka sok szépséget és mély érzelmeket tárolnak. Gyakran lehet őket olvasni a VGH Férfi és a Yuan Yuen Away Források című magazinokban. Nyelve modern, világos és egyszerű. Mivelhogy ezek a költemények gazdag érzelmeket rejtenek és mély értelmük van, sok külföldi tanár és diák kedveli őket, különösen elegáns stílusukért. Még a kínai kulturális múzeum igazgatója is kifejezte mély elismerését egy költeménnyel, amit Kínából, a tenger másik oldaláról küldött neki Tajvanba. Mindez mutatja, hogy ott is rajongva olvassák őket az emberek.

Egy kötetet <u>Életrend</u> címen adott ki Dr. Hsu 1991 júliusban. Mindkét nyelven, kínaiul és angolul hozza ez a kötet a verseit. Sok költőnek elküldte 34 országba azzal a céllal, hogy a kínai kulturát ezzel is terjessze.

Nagy megtiszteltetésnek tekintem, hogy Dr. Hsu több mint 200 versét olvashattam még mielőtt nyomtatásban is megjelent volna. Nagy hatást tett rám minden vers hagyományos szellemével és azzal, hogy még mindig megfelel korunk áramlatának is. Érzelmi gazdagságukat és mély ismeretanyagukat, ami ezekből a versekből sugárzik, nehéz lenne elfeledni. Egy válogatás ezekből a költeményekből most újra megjelenik nyomtatásban. Örülök, hogy ezt a néhány szót epilógusként megír hattam, amivel az volt a célom, hogy azoknak az olvasóknak, akik a kínai költészet iránt érdeklődnek, egy kis buzdítással szolgáljak.

1998 május 6-án　　　　　　　　Shih Yen-Chang
　　　　　　　　　　　　　　　　író